T0195684

In the Meantime

Bishop Timothy E. Criss

authorHOUSE®

AuthorHouse™
1663 Liberty Drive
Bloomington, IN 47403
www.authorhouse.com
Phone: 1 (800) 839-8640

Scripture quotations marked KJV are from the Holy Bible, King James Version (Authorized Version). First published in 1611. Quoted from the KJV Classic Reference Bible, Copyright © 1983 by The Zondervan Corporation.

Published by AuthorHouse 02/20/2017

ISBN: 978-1-5246-5886-1 (sc)
ISBN: 978-1-5246-5885-4 (e)

Print information available on the last page.

Any people depicted in stock imagery provided by Thinkstock are models, and such images are being used for illustrative purposes only. Certain stock imagery © Thinkstock.

This book is printed on acid-free paper.

ACKNOWLEDGEMENTS

I HONOR AND THANK GOD FOR ALL HE HAS DONE.

OF COURSE, I THANK MY WIFE SHERRY FOR BELIEVING IN ME THROUGHOUT ALL OF THIS MADNESS. WE'RE STILL STANDING. THANK YOU FOR TRUSTING ME WITH YOUR HEART; OUR DAUGHTERS TIMONY AND ARIENNE, THEIR HUSBANDS, AND OUR FOUR BEAUTIFUL GRANDCHILDREN FOR THEIR LOVE, SUPPORT, INSPIRATION AND ENCOURAGEMENT.

TO MY GREATER CITY OF REFUGE FAMILY, YOU ARE MY HEARTBEAT.

I CERTAINLY THANK MY FATHER, SUPT. ROBERT J. CRISS, SR. FOR BEING SUCH A STRONG EXAMPLE OF FAITH AND PERSEVERANCE IN MY LIFE, AND MY MOTHER, THE LATE EVANGELIST GEORGIANNA CRISS WHO CONSTANTLY GUARDED THE GIFT IN ME, MY BROTHERS AND SISTERS FOR LOOKING OUT FOR ME.

THANK YOU BISHOP TROTTER FOR YOUR SPIRITUAL GUIDANCE, AND FOR GIVING ME THE HONOR OF YOUR TRANSPARENCY. IT GAVE ME LIFE.

THANK YOU BISHOP GARNES FOR YOUR VOICE OF REASON.

THANK YOU SHARON, KAREN, CHRISTINA AND CAROLYN FOR KEEPING ME HEALTHY AND KEEPING ME ON SCHEDULE.

DEACON TOD...THANKS FOR YOUR PUSH TO GET THIS DONE.

THANKS TONY TIDWELL AND BRIAN LOFTON FOR YOUR MUSICAL GENIUS ON "STILL STANDING".

ALL OF YOU HAVE BEEN INCREDIBLE!

FOREWORD

IT WAS A LONG TIME COMING, BUT THIS FIRST BOOK BY MY SON, BISHOP TIMOTHY E. CRISS IS A MUST READ!!! EVERY LEADER AND EVERY BELIEVER WILL BE STRENGTHENED AS HE TAKES YOU ON A JOURNEY FULL OF THE REAL PITFALLS OF LIFE.

TIM'S TRANSPARENCY REGARDING WHAT ALL HAPPENED TO HIM, HIS FAMILY AND THE CHURCH IS A TESTIMONY OF RESTORATION FOR US ALL. PAGE BY PAGE, YOU WILL FEEL DIFFERENT EMOTIONS WHILE YOUR INNER BEING IS HEALED!

"IN THE MEANTIME" IS A MASTERPIECE, AND IT'S WELL WORTH THE READ.

I'M CERTAIN THIS BOOK WILL BECOME ONE OF
THE TREAURES IN YOUR LIBRARY.

BISHOP LARRY D. TROTTER
SWEET HOLY SPIRIT CHURCH
UTOPIA MUSIC GROUP
CHICAGO, IL

IN THE MEANTIME...

IT'S AN HONOR TO WRITE THIS NARRATIVE TO GOD'S GLORY AND FOR THE EDIFICATION OF EVERY READER.

I HAVE SO MUCH TO SAY THAT I DON'T KNOW WHERE TO START. FIRST OF ALL, I HUMBLY THANK GOD FOR THIS AWESOME OPPORTUINITY CALLED LIFE, AND IT'S GOOD TO BE LIVING IT TODAY. BY HIS GRACE, I AM A SURVIVOR, AND THERE'S JUST NO WAY I COULD HAVE MADE IT WITHOUT HIM. ALTHOUGH I THINK MY STORY IS REMARKABLE, I'M ASKING YOU TO DECIDE IF IT RESOUNDINGLY REMINDS YOU OF SOMEONE YOU KNOW, OR MAYBE EVEN YOU. AS YOU LOOK BACK OVER YOUR LIFE EXPOSURES, CERTAINLY YOU HAVE HAD AN EVENT, OR A PIECE OF JOURNEY, THAT ALMOST MADE YOU QUIT, LET GO, CHANGE DIRECTIONS, OR THROW IN THE TOWEL AND SAY "WHATEVA." THERE ARE THOSE OF US WHO HAVE HIDDEN SCARS THAT I HOPE THIS BOOK WILL HELP YOU SAY, THERE'S NO NEED TO HIDE THEM ANY LONGER. YOU'D BE SURPRISED WHO MIGHT HAVE A MATCHING SET.

ADMITTEDLY, IT TOOK ME A WHILE TO PUT THIS TOGETHER; BECAUSE HONESTLY, I WASN'T SURE I WAS PREPARED TO SHARE, MUCH LESS WRITE ABOUT MY VULNERABILITIES, MISTAKES, AND MISJUDGMENTS PUBLICLY. WE AS LEADERS

(CHIEF SERVANTS) LIKE TO SOMETIMES OFFER A "LARGER THAN LIFE" ACCOUNT FOR THINGS THAT REQUIRE A SIMPLE, GUTSY ADMISSION OF ERROR, OR EVEN DISASTROUS, TRAGIC FAILURES.

THIS BOOK IS NOT ABOUT HARBORING **BITTER**; IT IS HOWEVER ABOUT DISCOVERING STRATEGIES FOR WHAT IT TAKES TO GET **BETTER.** I WROTE THIS TO ASSURE THAT THE READER KNOWS THAT YOU REALLY CAN BOUNCE BACK AND RECOVER FROM YOUR MOST DIFFICULT AND CHALLENGING EXPERIENCES, AND THERE IS AN EXIT

FROM YOUR DARKEST OF DUNGEONS. IT PROBABLY WILL HURT THE WORST WHEN **YOU** DECIDE YOU ARE GOING TO LIVE THROUGH IT; THAT THIS WILL NOT BE THE FINAL CHAPTER OF YOUR STORY. THAT'S WHY IT IS LABELED A "MEAN TIME."

ONE THING THAT MAKES THIS NARRATIVE RATHER INTRIGUING IS THAT I'M NOT TELLING THIS STORY FROM THE PERSPECTIVE OF EVERYTHING BEING OVER, AND I'M AT THE FINISH LINE, BASKING IN TOTAL VICTORY, SINGING "HOW I GOT OVER"; INSTEAD, YOU GET TO WATCH AND WITNESS, IN LIVING COLOR, ASPECTS OF MY OVERCOMING PROCESS, BECAUSE I'M STILL A WORK IN RECOVERY. SO

LET'S WATCH THE STORY AS IT UNFOLDS, AND LET'S BE VICTORIOUS TOGETHER.

PLEASE ALLOW ME TO SHARE REALITY, MIXED WITH BLOOD, SWEAT, AND MANY TEARS. WHAT FOLLOWS IS RELEVANT, HAPPY, ENCOURAGING, AND HOPEFULLY INSPIRING. IT'S DEFINITELY ME, AND IT'S PROBABLY YOU, AND IT'S ANOINTED WITH THE OIL OF GOD'S WILL FOR US TO NEVER, EVER GIVE UP.

SO…I INVITE YOU FASTEN YOUR SEAT BELT, GRAB A CUP OF YOUR FAVORITE BEVERAGE, GET INTO YOUR EASY CHAIR IN FRONT OF THE FIREPLACE, OR FIND YOUR ASSIGNED SEAT ON YOUR FLIGHT, GRAB YOUR HIGHLIGHTER, AND GET READY TO BE CHALLENGED, AND ENCOURAGED. BECAUSE, IF YOU'VE KNOWN FOR A LONG TIME THAT YOU HAVE DIVINE PURPOSE IN YOUR LIFE, BUT COULD NEVER UNDERSTAND WHY, WITH ALL HIS DIRECTION, FAVOR, AND RESOURCES AT YOUR DISPOSAL, YOU KEEP COMING TO THIS PLACE THAT DOESN'T SEEM TO RESEMBLE THE PHOTOGRAPH OF YOUR DESTINY, YOUR PICTURE IS PROBABLY STILL DEVELOPING, AND YOU'RE PROBABLY EXPERIENCING A MEANTIME.

DON'T THINK YOUR ENCOUNTER IS "STRANGE" ACCORDING TO I PETER 4:12,13. HIS ENDEAVOR IS TO BRING US TO A PLACE WHERE WE CAN **REJOICE**, BECAUSE YOU HAVE BEEN INVITED TO THE **"PARTAKERS' PARTY."** SO TAKE JOY, AND

BE CONTENT ABOUT IT!!! YES, I SAID IT, AND YOU READ IT. YOU DON'T KNOW HOW HIGHLY FAVORED YOU ARE!

YOU'RE IN AN **AWESOME** PLACE, WITH A SELECT, CHOSEN GROUP; ON THE LAUNCH PAD POINTED TOWARDS GREATNESS. YOU'RE EARMARKED FOR EXPLOITS. (Daniel 11:32)

DON'T BE EMBARRASSED OR FEEL ISOLATED; **BE HONORED**. DON'T LET THIS OPPORTUNITY TO WORSHIP GOD PASS YOU BY. THE **MEAN TIME** MEANS THAT GOD IS **NOT FINISHED** WITH YOU. YOU'RE ON THE POTTER'S WHEEL, AND HE'S ADDING SOMETHING SPECIAL TO YOU...AND THAT'S SOMETHING TO BE ECSTATIC ABOUT.

I SINCERELY BELIEVE THAT WHAT YOU WILL READ IN THE NEXT SEVERAL PAGES WILL HELP YOU TO RECOGNIZE, PROCESS, ENDURE, THRIVE, AND TRIUMPH **"IN THE MEANTIME."**

Chapter 1

MEANTIME...DEFINED

ONE GENERALLY ACCEPTED DEFINITION IS: **FOR THE TIME BEING...FOR NOW... DURING THIS INTERVAL.**

ALTHOUGH THESE ATTEMPTS TO DEFINE THE TERM ARE WONDERFUL, AND COMMONLY ACCEPTED, THE TERM REALLY MEANS A LOT MORE:

WHILE YOU'RE WAITING, SOMETIMES ANXIOUSLY, FOR THE NEXT THING TO HAPPEN. IT'S THE TIME BEFORE THE NEXT CHANGE, SHIFT, MOVE, OR EXIT OR ENTRANCE; NOT PREPARED TO GO FORWARD, AND YOU'VE LIVED YOUR WHAT'S BEHIND YOU!

THE TIME DURING WHICH YOU FINALLY RECEIVE THE COMFORT OF UNDERSTANDING YESTERDAY AND HAVE A REVELATION FOR

TOMORROW, BUT YOUR TODAY IS HANGING BY A THIN THREAD OF UNCERTAINTY.

MEANTIMES SHOULD BE SOBERING, FILLED WITH INTROSPECTIONS, AND THOROUGH SELF EXAMINATIONS, SO AS TO PUT THE TRAIN BACK ON THE TRACK. THESE TIMES CAN BE FILLED WITH UNCERTAINTY AND IMBALANCE, YET THEY WILL BECOME THE STABILIZER FOR WHAT IS TO COME. MEANTIMES SHOULD BE VIEWED AS BELLWETHERS WHICH INDICATE SOMETHING TREMENDOUS IS ON THE HORIZON.

MEANTIMES CAN BE DIVISIVE, AND YET THE BRIDGE BETWEEN WHAT IS...AND WHAT IS TO COME; THE STRETCH OF HIGHWAY BETWEEN THE PROPHECY, AND THE MANIFESTATION OF THE SAME. INDEED, IT IS THE CONNECTION BETWEEN THE PROMISE, AND THE FULFILLMENT OF IT. AND ULTIMATELY, IT IS THE PROVING GROUND FOR YOUR FAITH.

MEANTIMES EXPOSE THE TRUTH OF WHAT YOU'RE MADE OF, AND ARE OFTEN JUST WHAT THE WORD SUGGESTS... IT IS...A **MEAN** TIME.

THESE TIMES HAVE THE PROPENSITY TO BE FRUSTRATING, CONFUSING, JOY-STEALING, MOMENTUM-CHANGING, OVERWHELMING, AND BREATHTAKING. OFTEN, THEY MAKE YOU FEEL LIKE THROWING IN THE TOWEL, AND MAKE YOU WONDER IF YOU EVER HEARD GOD'S

VOICE. THEY IMPACT YOUR PRAYERS, AND CAN CAUSE YOU TO FEEL INADEQUATE AND IL-EQUIPPED TO CONTINUE WHAT YOU STARTED.

HOWEVER, PAUL, THE APOSTLE GIVES A POWERFUL, EYE-OPENING REMINDER ABOUT HOW TO REGARD MEANTIMES: "FOR OUR LIGHT AFFLICTION, **WHICH IS BUT FOR A MOMENT**, WORKETH IN US A FAR MORE AND EXCEEDING, AND ETERNAL WEIGHT OF GLORY"...IN SHORT, IF YOU CAN ENDURE IT, WHAT YOU RECEIVE FROM THE EXPERIENCE FAR OUTWEIGHS WHAT YOU CONTRIBUTED WHILE YOU WERE IN IT, AND THEY BRING GLORIOUS AND ETERNAL REWARDS.

PLEASE KEEP IN MIND THAT GOD CAREFULLY ORCHESTRATES IN HIS DIVINE SCHEDULE FOR YOUR GOOD TIMES AND MEANTIMES, AND HE ALLOWS THEM FOR OUR EDIFICATION AND GROWTH. YOUR STEPS ARE ORDERED BY THE LORD. THESE TIMES, IN FACT ARE EMPLOYED TO HELP US BECOME SHAPEABLE IN GOD'S WILL, SINCE ALL THINGS WORK TOGETHER FOR OUR GOOD, ACCORDING TO HIS PURPOSE...**ROMANS 8:28.** HE'S TOO POWERFUL, TOO STRATEGIC, TOO PRECISE, TOO INTENTIONAL, AND TOO WISE TO LET THINGS HAPPEN COINCIDENTALLY, HAPHAZARDLY OR ACCIDENTALLY. HE'S TOO FOCUSED ON OUR EVERY STEP NOT TO HAVE GOALS SET FOR US TO ACHIEVE WHICH, ARE

DESIGNED TO BRING OUT THE BEST IN US, AND GLORIFY HIM. **SO TAKE COURAGE**. THERE WILL BE TIMES YOU ARE GOING TO WONDER WHAT GLORY GOD CAN POSSIBLY GET FROM THIS SEASON IN YOUR LIFE. CONFLICT, CONTROVERSY, AND ADVERSITY SHOULD NOW PROBABLY BE

VIEWED FROM A DIFFERENT, MORE POSITIVE PERSPECTIVE, WHEN WE UNDERSTAND THAT MEANTIMES DON'T NECESSARILY SHOW UP BECAUSE SOMETHING IS WRONG; OFTEN THEY SHOW UP BECAUSE SOMETHING IS RIGHT, **BUT ALWAYS TO PERFECT US.**

IF WE ARE SUPPOSED TO GLORY IN TRIBULATIONS (ROMANS 5:3), MAYBE WE REALLY NEED TO ADJUST OUR PERSPECTIVE OF THE WHOLE TRIAL AND TRIBULATIONS PIECE. I KNOW THIS SOUNDS CRAZY, BUT MAYBE THE GREATEST PRAISE SHOULD HAPPEN WHEN WE GO INTO THE TEST, INSTEAD OF WAITING 'TIL WE COME OUT!!!

ALSO LET ME ADD THAT WE PROBABLY NEED TO CONSIDER HOW WE TREAT THOSE WHO ARE IN THE THROWS OF ADVERSITY, BUT TRYING TO MAKE IT THROUGH. CONSIDER THAT MAYBE IT WOULD BE MORE MEANINGFUL TO CELEBRATE THEM WHILE THEY ARE IN THE MIDST OF MEANTIME, INSTEAD OF WHEN (IF) THEY MAKE

IT THROUGH IT. SOME FOLKS DON'T SURVIVE!
JUST FOOD FOR THOUGHT.

MEANTIMES ARE CRITICAL; **BECAUSE HOW
YOU NAVIGATE THEM WILL ULTIMATELY
DETERMINE YOUR NEXT STEPS, AND
QUITE FRANKLY, YOUR FUTURE, AND THE
FULFILLMENT OF YOUR DESTINY. IT'S
PROBABLY MOST PAINFUL WHEN YOU DECIDE
YOU'RE GOING TO HOLD ON THROUGH YOUR
MEANTIME, SINCE IT'S GOING TO COST YOU
TO STAY.** IF YOU DON'T DEVELOP YOUR FAITH,
PATIENCE, PRAYER CONNECTION, FOCUS, AND
KEEP MOVING, MEANTIMES CAN LAST LONGER
THAN YOU, AND ROB YOU OF YOUR **"LIFE"** TIME.

Chapter 2

SO...WE GREW AND WE GREW

WE WERE THE BLAINE STREET CHURCH. AND
FOR THE "CONSERVATIVE" PEORIA AREA, OUR
JOURNEY WAS NOT TYPICAL.

APPROXIMATELY 12 PEOPLE WERE ATTENDING
BIBLE STUDY AND 30 ATTENDING SUNDAY
MORNING SERVICE. THE ROOF LEAKED, THE
BATHROOMS WERE IN DISREPAIR, AND WE HAD
TO OPEN THE WINDOWS DURING THE SUMMER
TO LET MORE HOT AIR IN, BUT THE SOULFUL
SOUNDS ATTACHED THEMSELVES TO THE
WIND AND FILLED THE NEIGHBORHOOD AIR.
THE SURROUNDING HOUSES BEGAN TO EMPTY
EVERY SUNDAY AROUND THE WORSHIP HOUR,
AS THE PEOPLE FILLED THE HARD WOODEN
PEWS. THE WORD BEGAN TO SPREAD AND GOD
FAVORED US WITH REMARKABLE INCREASE. AT
FIRST WE HAD A FEW SINGERS WHO GATHERED
AROUD THE ORGANIST QUARTET- STYLE AND
THEN WE GREW A FIERCE CHOIR THAT SANG

UNTIL IT SEEMS THE HEAVENS SHOOK. WE EVEN RECORDED OUR FIRST CD, AND OUR PROJECT BLESSED PEOPLE ACROSS THE NATION.

WE PROVIDED COMMUNITY ASSISTANCE FOR THOSE SEEKING JOBS AND HOUSING, MALE MENTORING PROGRAMS, PANTRIES, COMPUTER EDUCATION, CHILD EDUCATION SERVICES, ETC. SINCE WE DIDN'T HAVE ADEQUATE PARKING, WE GAINED SPECIAL PERMISSION FROM THE POLICE DEPARTMENT TO PARK PRETTY MUCH WHEREVER WE COULD UNTIL THIS COULD BE REMEDIED.

WE PURCHASED PROPERTY IN THE NEIGHBORHOOD AND INSTALLED PARKING LOTS, FIXED THE LEAKING ROOF, REMODELED THE BATHROOMS CHILDCARE AND CLASSROOM AREAS, PURCHASED TRANSPORTATION, REMODELED AN ADJACENT HOUSE FOR THE HOMELESS, AND ANOTHER HOME FOR THOSE RECOVERING FROM ADDICTIONS, FOUND JOBS AND TECHNICALLY AND PHYSICALLY PREPARED THE UNEMPLOYED FOR POSSIBLE WORK OPPORTUNITIES.

WE HAD TO BEGIN HAVING TWO SERVICES ON SUNDAYS TO KEEP PACE WITH OUR CONGREGATION'S GROWTH, AND THE CLASSROOMS BECAME QUICKLY OVERCROWDED FOR BIBLE STUDIES AND NEW MEMBER CLASSES. WE WERE ONE OF THE

FIRST CHURCHES IN PEORIA (THAT I'M AWARE OF) WHO IMPLEMENTED VALET PARKING, SINCE PARKING WAS SUCH A PREMIUM IN OUR NEIGHBORHOOD. WE RAISED MONEY FOR A "FEED THE CHILDREN" CAMPAIGN, WHICH FED HUNDREDS OF FAMILIES DURING THE HOLIDAYS.

LIKE ANY PASTOR/MANAGER/CEO (PER BISHOP ERIC D. GARNES), I STARTED LOOKING FOR WAYS TO ACCOMMODATE OUR BURGEONING GROWTH. WE FOUND AN ABANDONED DEPARTMENT STORE JUST BLOCKS AWAY THAT WAS EARMARKED FOR PARTIAL DEMOLITION, TO BE RENOVATED AS A BANK. AS THE BANK SHOWED ME THEIR BLUEPRINTS AND PLANS, I PRESSED UPON THEM WHY WE NEEDED THAT SPACE. WE COULD REMAIN IN OUR COMMUNITY, AND CONTINUE TO MAKE AN IMPACT RIGHT WHERE WE WERE MOST NEEDED. THEY SAID WE OBVIOUSLY ALREADY HAVE PLANS, BUT IF WE CAN LOCATE AN ALTERNATIVE FOR OUR BANK EXPANSION, WE WILL CONSIDER YOUR REQUEST. IN JUST A FEW WEEKS, GOD PROVIDED ANOTHER PROPERTY FOR THEM, SO WE PURCHASED THE 52,000 SQUARE FOOT PROJECT WHICH LATER WOULD BE RECOGNIZED THROUGHOUT THE CITY OF PEORIA, AND AWARDED AS ONE OF THE MOST BEAUTIFUL TRANSFORMATIONS IN OUR CITY.

WE WORKED FEVERISHLY DURING THE WEEK, AND THEN CLEANED THE SANCTUARY AND DUSTED THE RENTED CHAIRS ON SATURDAYS SO WE COULD HAVE SERVICE ON SUNDAY. THEN ON MONDAYS, WE PULLED OUT THE SAWS, THE DRYWALL, PAINT BRUSHES, AND THE HAMMERS, AND WENT RIGHT BACK TO WORK. SOMETIMES WE WORKED ON THE EXTERIOR WHILE WE WORKED ON THE INTERIOR, WHICH OFTEN CREATED JOBS FOR OUR UNEMPLOYED CHURCH MEMBERS AND THE DISENFRANCHISED IN OUR COMMUNITY.

IT WAS TRULY A LABOR OF LOVE, BECAUSE THE PEOPLE HAD A MIND TO WORK. WHAT GOD WAS DOING FOR US AND THROUGH US WAS SIMPLY PHENOMENAL.

THIS FACILITY PROVIDED SPACE FOR A SANCTUARY, CLASS ROOMS, TWO ELEVATORS, 13,000 SQUARE FEET FOR COMMUNITY BUSINESSES, CHILD CARE, OFFICE SPACE, ADDITIONAL RESTROOMS, MORE THAN ADEQUATE PARKING, A BAPTISMAL AREA, A FELLOWSHIP HALL, ETC. IT WAS EVERYTHING A BUSTLING CONGREGATION COULD ASK FOR.

WE ESTABLISHED AN ENTREPRENEURIAL OPPORTUNITY ON SITE FOR SMALL BUSINESSES WHICH ATTRACTED A LOCAL BANK, WHICH MOVED INTO OUR FACILITY AND ANCHORED US, A NOVELTY SHOP, A CELL PHONE STORE,

A TAX PREPARATION OFFICE, A BEAUTY SHOP, A FED EX SHIPPING CENTER, A MEN'S STORE, AND MORE. OUR EFFORTS CAUGHT THE EYE OF THE SUMMER LEADERSHIP INSTITUTE AT THE **HARVARD DIVINITY SCHOOL**, AND I WAS INVITED TO COME, ATTEND THE CLASSES, AND SHARE WHAT WE WERE ATTEMPTING TO DO, SINCE OUR CITY HAD BEEN DESIGNATED AS HAVING THE FEWEST NUMBER OF AFRICAN-AMERICAN AND WOMEN-OWNED BUSINESSES FOR A CITY ITS SIZE IN **THE UNITED STATES OF AMERICA... IN THE WHOLE NATION, Y'ALL!.**

MOST RECENTLY, PEORIA, IL WAS ALSO NAMED THE WORST CITY IN THE NATION FOR AFRICAN-AMERICANS TO LIVE, BASED ON UNEMPLOYMENT, EDUCATION, HOUSING DATA, ETC. IN ALL OF THESE UNITED STATES OF AMERICA!

ANYWAY, WE WERE THE BUZZ OF THE CITY AS WE FILLED NEARLY EVERY SQUARE FOOT OF THIS BUILDING...AND **WE GREW, AND WE GREW.**

Chapter 3

A PASTOR'S DREAM

UNDERSTANDING THE CYCLES OF MINISTRY AS A PREACHER'S KID, AND ONE INVOLVED IN YEARS OF PREPARATORY EDUCATION AND MINISTRY, WE STARTED GETTING SETTLED INTO THE RIGORS OF OUR NEW RESPONSIBILITIES AS CARE GIVERS FOR GOD'S PEOPLE.

WE ESTABLISHED STRUCTURES FOR TRAININGS AND SUPPORT SYSTEMS DESIGNED TO MAKE OUR FOUNDATIONS STRONG FOR THE ENTIRE FAMILY. IT WAS IMPORTANT THAT WE UNDERSTOOD WHAT THE DYNAMICS OF OUR FAMILIES WERE, SO WE MOBILIZED RESOURCES AROUND US TO MAKE US RELEVANT AND IMPACTFUL. I WANTED **EVERYONE** WHO ATTENDED OUR MINISTRY TO BE WELL EQUIPPED TO LIVE A VICTORIOUS, MEANINGFUL LIFE (**JOHN 10:10**).

OUR CHURCH HAD BEEN BLESSED WITH A

PLETHORA OF MINISTERS AND QUALIFIED TEACHERS, AND EXPERIENCED STAFF MEMBERS WHO I BELIEVED, AT THAT TIME, UNDERSTOOD THE NECESSITY OF SACRIFICE, AND WERE COMMITTED TO OUR BLOSSOMING VISION. GOD GAVE US FAVOR WITH FINANCERS AND CITY OFFICIALS, AND WE WERE DILIGENT, AND FRUGAL WITH WHAT HAD BEEN ENTRUSTED TO US BY GOD.

OUR MINISTRY WAS THE PICTURE OF GOD'S TRANSFORMATION POWER; JUST AS WE WERE TRANSFORMING A PREVIOUS DEPARTMENT STORE INTO A MULTI-USE FACILITY, GOD WAS TRANSFORMING US INTO A COMMUNITY OF FORMIDABLE, EFFECTIVE SOLDIERS, WHO WERE UNIFIED FOR THE CAUSE OF THE KINGDOM. OUR WEEKLY SERVICES WERE CHARISMATIC, HOLY GHOST-CHARGED, AND POWERFUL, AND OUR 7 A.M. SATURDAY

MORNING PRAYER SERVICES WITNESSED PEOPLE COMING IN FROM OFF THE STREETS AFTER LEAVING THE CLUBS IN THE WEE HOURS OF THE MORNING TO RECEIVE SALVATION. WE WERE EXPERIENCING A **MOVE OF GOD**.

NO LONGER CALLED THE BLAINE STREET CHURCH, WE WERE BECOMING WHAT I SAW IN MY TIME OF VISITATION FROM THE LORD, **A CITY OF REFUGE**; A PLACE WHERE PEOPLE COULD COME AND HAVE A DIFFERENT "CHURCH"

EXPERIENCE AND CHRIST ENCOUNTER. THEY COULD COME AND NOT BE JUDGED BY THEIR PASTS, AND FOCUS ON BEING THAT NEW CREATURE IN CHRIST; GET A FRESH START AND ESCAPE THOSE CONDEMNING FORMER TRAPS OF THEIR LIFE EXPERIENCES.

I BELIEVED WE HAD CAPTURED THE HEARTBEAT OF GOD, AS WE STRIVED TO BECOME A MINISTRY IN THE HEART OF THE CITY, WITH THE CITY IN ITS HEART; A PLACE WHERE THERE WOULD NOT BE A NEED THAT MINISTRY COULD NOT SOMEHOW ADDRESS**... A PASTOR'S DREAM... RIGHT?**

$\mathcal{Chapter}$ 4

THE NIGHTMARE BEGINS

DURING A MINISTERS' MEETING, A FEW OF MY STAFF MEMBERS COMMENTED THAT SOME OF OUR MEMBERS HAD EXPRESSED SOME CONCERNS REGARDING SOME IMPORTANT ISSUES WITHIN OUR CHURCH ADMINISTRATION (WHICH WAS NOT UNCOMMON). HOWEVER, MY REAL CONCERN WAS WHY THESE PEOPLE, WITH WHOM I THOUGHT I HAD REAL RELATIONSHIP, ALLEGEDLY INFORMED MY STAFF MEMBERS OF THEIR UNHAPPINESS, AND NOT ME. I BELIEVED I HAD PROVEN MYSELF TO BE A STRONG COMMUNICATOR, AND UTILIZED AN OPEN DOOR POLICY WITH OUR CONGREGANTS. I WAS NOT AN **IVORY TOWER** LEADER, AND YOU DIDN'T HAVE TO GO THROUGH THREE PEOPLE TO GET TO ME. ALTHOUGH I WAS A BUSY PASTOR, I WAS VERY APPROACHABLE, AND WELCOMED OUR PEOPLE'S COMMENTS, OR CRITICISMS. I SOON DEDUCED THAT THERE HAD BEEN

SOME MEETINGS PRIOR TO THE MEETING I WAS HAVING, AND THE SAD SAGA OF OUR CHURCH SPLIT HAD BEGUN.

THERE WAS SUCH AN UNDERCURRENT OF BETRAYAL WHICH HAD BEEN IN OPERATION FOR SOME TIME THAT IT LITERALLY MADE MY HEAD SPIN. HOW COULD I NOT BE COGNIZANT OF WHAT WAS REALLY HAPPENING BEFORE NOW?

THINGS HAD BEEN SECRETLY SET IN MOTION THAT WERE ABOUT TO OCCUR THAT I COULDN'T PREVENT AT THIS POINT. I BECAME PASTOR/PLATE-SPINNER DURING THIS INTERVAL, JUST TRYING TO KEEP THINGS FROM CRASHING. I FOUND MYSELF WATCHING THE DEVASTATION IN THE PEW, AS I TRIED TO MAINTAIN SOME TYPE OF ORDER FROM BEHIND THE PODIUM.

AS I WATCHED OUR NUMBERS DWINDLE, AND WATCHED THE QUIET AND SOMETIMES BEFUDDLED FACES OF OUR PEOPLE, MY TRANSPARENCY PROBABLY BECAME ANNOYING. I WAS AS, IF NOT MORE, SURPRISED AS THEY WERE BY THESE EVENTS. IN FACT, MANY OF THEM KNEW MORE THAN I DID, BUT DIDN'T (WOULDN'T) SHARE IT WITH ME IN A TIMELY MANNER DURING WHICH I COULD HAVE REACTED. THAT WAS SO VERY PAINFUL.

I CONTINUED TO OFFER ENCOURAGEMENT TO OUR PEOPLE, BECAUSE I THOUGHT THAT'S

WHAT I WAS SUPPOSED TO DO. (EERILY, I WONDERED IF THIS WAS THE WAY THOSE MUSICIANS FELT WHO WERE PLAYING MUSIC FOR THE PASSENGERS OF THE TITANIC WHILE IT WAS SINKING).

BISHOP T.D. JAKES OFFERS ENCOURAGEMENTS WITH REGARDS TO LEADING WHILE BLEEDING, BUT WE WERE HEMORRHAGING BEYOND IMAGINATION.

IN RETROSPECT, I WASN'T HONEST ABOUT MY FEELINGS, AND WASN'T DEALING WITH THE BRIGHT RED ELEPHANT IN THE ROOM. I WAS NO LONGER SURE WHO I WAS TRYING TO IMPRESS WITH MY PERSEVERANCE; GOD, MY FAMILY, OR THE PEOPLE; (MAYBE ALL THREE). HOWEVER, THERE SEEMED TO BE NO REWARD, **BECAUSE I COULDN'T FOOL ME.**

I WOULD LIKE TO PUNCH THE MIS-INFORMED, SUPPOSED POET WHO COINED THE PHRASE "STICKS AND STONES MAY BREAK MY BONES, BUT WORDS WILL NEVER HURT ME." **HE LIED**. MY QUESTION THEN BECAME, WHY IS MY HEART SO SHATTERED, AND MY EMOTIONS SO RIPPED APART? I WOULD RATHER HAVE SUFFERED A PHYSICAL BEAT-DOWN THAN TO FEEL THE WAY I DID. I FELT **DESERTED, EMBARRASSED, ANGRY, AND DEPRESSED**, **(D.E.A.D.);** AND I'M SURE THOSE WHO WERE CLOSE AND LOVED ME FELT THE SAME WAY.

OUR SPLIT WAS SUDDEN, AND HARD; IT SPLIT FAMILIES IN THEIR LOYALTY AND LOVE TOWARDS ME AND OUR MINISTRY.

NOTHING IN MY VAST STUDY RESOURCES, BIBLICAL/PASTORAL TRAINING, INSPIRATIONAL SERMONS I'D HEARD, BUSINESS DEALINGS, SEMINARS, CONVENTIONS, CONFERENCES, CONVOCATIONS, OR SIMPLY CONVERSATIONS WITH MY DAD OR OTHER EXPERIENCED PASTORS COULD HAVE PREPARED ME FOR WHAT A GROUP OF TONGUE-TALKING, HEAVEN-BOUND, BAPTIZED BELIEVERS HAD JUST PERPETRATED IN THE NAME OF JESUS. I FELT LIKE I WAS IN RUINS. (EXCUSE ME, MY BANDAGES ARE SEEPING).

WAS THIS THE END OF MY MINISTERIAL CAREER, I ASKED GOD? IF THIS IS THE "FELLOWSHIP OF YOUR SUFFERING," THEN WILL I ALSO WITNESS THE "POWER OF YOUR RESURRECTION"? **(PHILLIPIANS 3:10).**

A PECULIAR SEASON HAD MADE ITS ARRIVAL**; I WAS AT THE PRECIPICE OF MY MEANTIME.**

Chapter 5

MY WORMS HAD AN APETITE…

SO, AS WE CONTINUED DOWN A PATH TO REGROUP, CALCULATE OUR LOSSES AND REBUILD, I REALIZED THAT A LOT OF HEALING HAD TO TAKE PLACE, FROM THE PULPIT TO THE ENTRANCE OF OUR CHURCH DOORS. I SPENT A LOT OF TIME, UNDER GOD'S DIRECTION, SETTING A COURSE TO STRENGTHEN WHAT REMAINED. I WAS CAREFUL ABOUT WHO I INVITED TO SPEAK TO OUR PEOPLE, AS I LEARNED TONS OF INFORMATION BY LISTENING TO OUR CONGREGANTS. MANY OF THEM HAD BEEN WOUNDED, BUT THEY STAYED TO BE SUPPORTIVE, AND TO HEAR WHAT GOD WOULD SAY NEXT. THANKFULLY, THEY REMAINED FAITHFULLY ATTACHED TO OUR VISION.

AND THEN... THE OTHER SHOE DROPPED

AS I WAS SITTING IN MY OFFICE AT THE CHURCH ONE MORNING, I RECEIVED A VERY DISTURBING CALL FROM OUR BANK. THE BANK OFFICIAL GREETED ME VERY POLITELY AND BEGAN TO EXPLAIN TO ME THAT THE BALLOON ON OUR LOAN WAS APPROACHING ITS MATURITY, AND THE BANKS POSITION WAS TO DEMAND THE REST OF THE BALANCE BY A SPECIFIC DATE.

HE SAID TO ME THAT THEIR BANK NO LONGER WANTED TO BE IN THE CHURCH OR NOT-FOR PROFIT LENDING BUSINESS. HE EXPLAINED THAT THERE WAS NOT A PROBLEM WITH DELINQUENT PAYMENTS, OR ANYTHING OF THAT SORT. THIS WAS THEIR EXIT STRATEGY ON OUR LOAN, AND SEVERAL OTHERS. WELL, I SIMPLY TOLD HIM THAT WE DIDN'T HAVE THAT KIND OF MONEY, SO HE SUGGESTED THAT WE FIND SOME OTHER BANK TO REFINANCE US.

OUR LEGAL COUNCIL SAID THAT THE BANK WAS JUSTIFIED CONTRACTUALLY IN WHAT THEY WERE ASKING OF US. AT THAT TIME, WE REALLY DIDN'T SEE A REAL ISSUE SINCE WE HAD GOOD EQUITY IN OUR FACILITY BASED ON THE LATEST APPRAISAL INFORMATION, AND WE HAD A GOOD PAYMENT HISTORY, SO THE SEARCH BEGAN.

ALL OF THIS STARTED HAPPENING WHEN

MANY BANKS WERE UNDER INTENSE SCRUTINY FOR FRAUDULENT LENDING PRACTICES, AND SEVERAL WERE BEING CLOSED ACROSS THE COUNTRY. WE TOOK OUR REQESTS TO NEARLY EVERY BANK, CREDIT UNION, AND MORTGAGE COMPANY YOU COULD IMAGINE WITHIN A 150 MILE RADIUS OF OUR CITY. EVERYONE WANTED A NEW SET OF APPRAISALS, SURVEYS, FINANCIALS, ETC.; ALL OF WHICH WERE COSTLY TO OBTAIN, YET NO ONE WOULD APPROVE US. AT FIRST, OUR BANK WAS PATIENT, BUT THEN THEY GREW A LOT LESS UNDERSTANDING, AS WAS DEMONSTRATED WHEN MY WIFE AND I WERE FORCED TO LEAVE OUR LOVELY HOME, AND OUR CARS WERE REPOSSESSED. OUR TWO VEHICLES AND OUR HOME HAD BEEN TAKEN, AND THE BANKS ATTORNEY SAID THEY HAD A RIGHT TO RECOVER WHATEVER THEY COULD TO SATISFY OUR DEBT FROM THE CHURCH (YES, THIS REALLY HAPPENED, AND I'M BEING EXTREMELY SEDATE WITH MY EXPLANATION).

I HAD BEEN WAITING FOR THE TITLE TO ONE OF THE VEHICLES, BECAUSE ITS BALANCE HAD BEEN **PAID IN FULL**. THE OTHER VEHICLE'S PAYMENTS WERE TAKEN FROM AN ACCOUNT DIRECTLY SO AS TO INSURE ITS TIMELINESS. MONIES REMAINED IN THE ACCOUNT BECAUSE THE BANK WOULD NOT ACCEPT PAYMENTS ANY LONGER. INSTEAD, THEY DEMANDED THE ENTIRE BALANCE, NOT THE REGULARLY

SCHEDULED PAYMENT. WE WERE INFORMED
SHORTLY THEREAFTER THAT OUR VEHICLES
WERE SOLD AT AUCTION. FORTUNATELY, MY
WIFE AND I WERE ABLE TO PURCHASE OTHER
VEHICLES IMMEDIATELY, FOR WHICH WE ARE
ETERNALLY GRATEFUL.

OUR MORTGAGE BROKER HAD IDENTIFIED A
PRIVATE LENDER WHO AGREED TO REFINANCE
US. WE WERE APPROVED AND HAD BEEN GIVEN
A CLOSING DATE, DOCUMENTS, CLOSING
LOCATION, ETC.; ALL OF WHICH FELL INSIDE
OF THE BANK'S DEADLINE. THIS FINALLY WAS A
BRIGHT LIGHT SHINING ON THIS DARK ROAD,
OR SO WE THOUGHT.

TWO DAYS BEFORE CLOSING, THE OWNER
OF THE MORTGAGE COMPANY DIED OF AN
APPARENT HEART ATTACK, AND ALL CLOSINGS
(OURS AND SEVEN OTHER BORROWERS) WERE,
AT BEST, FROZEN, UNTIL FURTHER NOTICE
BY THE FAMILY OF THE DECEASED. IN AN
ACT OF DESPERATION, WE SPOKE TO A VERY
WEALTHY FRIEND OF MINE WHO SAID THAT
HE AND HIS BUSINESS PARTNERS WOULD
INTERVENE AND BRIDGE THE GAP UNTIL THE
MORTGAGE COMPANY CAME THROUGH. AFTER
WE PROVIDED ALL THE DOCUMENTATION HE
REQUESTED, HE AND HIS PARTNERS HAD A LAST
MINUTE CHANGE OF HEART, AND DENIED OUR
URGENT REQUEST. **OUR TIME AND OPTIONS**

HAD JUST RAN OUT. THERE WAS NO REASON FOR US TO BELIEVE THAT ONE OF THESE RESOURCES WOULD NOT PAN OUT FOR US, SO WE HADN'T MADE PLANS TO MOVE 52,000 SQUARE FEET OF STUFF.

WHEN OUR BANK HEARD THE NEWS OF THE OWNER'S DEATH, THEY SAID, WE CAN'T WAIT ANY LONGER; WE NEED THE KEYS TO YOUR BUILDING; SO WE SURRENDERED THEM.

MY WORMS CERTAINLY HAD VORACIOUS APETITES; WOULDN'T YOU AGREE (JOEL CHAPTER 2:25)?

SO NOW, LET'S TRY TO SUM THIS UP...WE HAD LOST THE BUILDING WHICH HOUSED OUR DRUG TREATMENT CENTER WHICH TREATED 150 PATIENTS PER DAY, OUR TRANSITIONAL HOME FOR RECOVERING ADDICTS, OUR BUSINESSES LIKE OUR FED EX SHIPPING CENTER AND OUR CALL CENTER WHICH WERE HOUSED INSIDE OF OUR FACILITY, OUR PERSONAL HOME, OUR CARS; AND OF COURSE, OUR CHURCH BUILDING. WE LOST CLOSE FRIENDS, AND STRONG, MEANINGFUL RELATIONSHIPS WERE RIPPED APART, AND OTHER SUBSTANTIAL INTANGIBLES THINGS THAT ONE JUST CAN'T MEASURE. I LOST A GREAT DEAL OF MOMENTUM, DESIRE, AND ENERGY. I FELT AS THOUGH I HAD LOST MY IDENTITY, AND MY JOY.

AND IF THAT'S NOT ENOUGH, MY FAMILY PHYSICIAN HAD JUST DIAGNOSED ME WITH DIABETES. I LITERALLY THOUGHT I WAS LOSING MY MIND; THE BANK MIGHT AS WELL TOOK THAT TOO.

I CAN'T EXPLAIN IT, BUT ONLY BY THE GRACE OF GOD WERE WE KEPT. THIS WAS A VERY SOBERING TIME; YET, IN MY PRIVATE TIME, I KNEW THAT GOD STILL EXPECTED, AND DESERVED MY PRAISE.

DAVID, WHAT HAD YOU EXPERIENCED WITH GOD, WHEN YOU SAID "I WILL BLESS THE LORD AT ALL TIMES, AND HIS PRAISE SHALL CONTINUALLY BE IN MY MOUTH" (PSALMS 34?). HE PROBABLY WAS EXPRESSING HIS DETERMINATION TO BE STEDFAST IN GOOD TIMES, AND WHILE FACING THE AMBIGUITY OF HIS MEANTIMES.

I FOUND MYSELF IN WHAT COMPARES TO A SURGICAL, STERILE FIELD; IN A PLACE WHERE NOT JUST ANYBODY WAS QAUALIFIED, EXPERIENCED, OR CAREFUL ENOUGH TO OPERATE ON MY HEART, OR MINISTER TO MY CONDITION. AND WHAT WAS I SUPPOSED TO SAY TO OUR CONGREGATION? HOW COULD I ENCOURAGE THEM TO STAY? MORE IMPORTANTLY, WHAT WOULD I SAY TO MY FAMILY?

I CALLED MY WIFE AND OUR TWO DAUGHTERS TO THE CHURCH AFTER I TURNED IN THE KEYS AND WE HAD A HEART TO HEART TALK. IT WAS VERY DIFFICULT, BUT I TOLD THEM:

"ALTHOUGH I CAN'T EXPLAIN WHAT IS HAPPENING, OR WHY, I JUST KNOW THAT GOD DIDN'T FAIL US; SO LET'S NOT BE BITTER TOWARDS HIM... HE'S UP TO SOMETHING, AND I WANT TO FIND OUT WHAT IT IS. I KNOW HE DIDN'T BRING US HERE TO LEAVE US IN RUINS!

LET'S TRUST HIM TO REVEAL HIS PLANS FOR US, AND RESTORE US; BECAUSE THAT'S HIS PROMISE, AND HE'S NO SHORTER THAN HIS PROMISE. HE HAS NEVER FAILED."

NO REST FOR THE WEARY...

AFTER WE CRIED AND PRAYED TOGETHER, THEY LEFT, AND I MADE PHONE CALLS TO OUR BROTHERS AND CHURCH OFFICIALS, AND WE WENT TO U-HAUL AND RENTED TRUCKS. WE BEGAN THE ARDUOUS PROCESS OF OUR MOVE. OUR SANCTUARY CHAIRS, SOUND SYSTEM, SPEAKERS, MUSICAL EQUIPMENT, OFFICE FURNITURE, BUSINESS EQUIPMENT, WALL HANGINGS, LAMPS,PERSONAL EFFECTS...IT ALL HAD TO BE PACKED AND MOVED IMMEDIATELY. A DEAR PASTOR FRIEND OF MINE OPENED THE STORAGE AREA OF HIS CHURCH, AND MY COUSIN LET ME BORROW A STORAGE FACILITY

SHE HAD AVAILABLE, AND WE WENT TO WORK. I'M FOREVER GRATEFUL FOR THOSE WHO MADE THEMSELVES AVAILABLE DURING OUR TIME OF NEED. **GOD BLESS YOU!**

INTERESTINGLY, SOME OF MY PASTOR (SUPPOSED) FRIENDS, AND OTHERS CAME BY WITH THEIR PICK-UP TRUCKS, CIRCLING OUR BUILDING AND ASKING IF THERE WERE ITEMS WE WANTED TO SELL OR GIVE AWAY, TO WHICH I ASKED **"ARE YOU KIDDING ME RIGHT NOW?"**

MEANTIMES OFTEN EXPOSE WHO REALLY HAS YOUR BACK; AND THE TRUTH OF THAT DISCOVERY CAN BE DEAFENING.

MY MOUTH WAS DRY FROM TALKING, MY EAR WAS SORE FROM LISTENING, MY HEAD WAS HURTING FROM WORRY, AND MY EYES WERE RED AND DRY FROM CRYING. I JUST KNEW THAT LIFE AS I HAD KNOWN IT HAD COME TO AN END. THE WHISPERING WONDERS CARRIED THE WORD OF OUR WOES EVERYWHERE. THE INTERNET WAS NO MATCH FOR THE PEOPLES' FRENZY TO SPREAD THE WORD.

I WAS SO BUSY LOOKING AT WHAT LEFT THAT I ALMOST LOST FOCUS ON WHAT STAYED. WE HAD BECOME FACEBOOK FURY,

EMAIL EXTRAORDINAIRES, AND THE THREE POINTS AND THE CONCLUSION OF SOME

PASTOR'S SUNDAY MORNING SERMONS. THIS WAS INCREDIBLE!

HOW WAS I SUPPOSE TO UNDERSTAND THAT GOD WAS PREPARING ME FOR A SHIFT THAT I NEVER COULD HAVE IMAGINED; TO BE CONTENT WITH WHAT I HAD LEFT? RIGHT NOW, IT WAS A COME-UP TO HAVE JUST ENOUGH.

I THOUGHT, HOW IN THE WORLD CAN THIS GIVE YOU GLORY? I FELT STRANDED BECAUSE I LOVED GOD TOO MUCH TO JUST WALK AWAY. AFTER ALL, HE HAD NEVER LEFT ME BEFORE; EVER BEEN THERE?

EVERYTHING THAT COULD BE VIOLATED WAS; EVERY FENCE HAD BEEN BREACHED. THE PROVERBIAL WATERS WERE COMING UP AND OVER THE WALL AND RISING.

I REALLY NEEDED GOD TO MOVE FOR ME AS WAS DESCRIBED IN ISAIAH 59:19…WHEN THE ENEMY COMES, LIKE A FLOOD THE SPIRIT OF THE LORD WILL LIFT UP A STANDARD AGAINST MY ENEMY.

AS I SAT IN THE GALLERIA OF OUR BUILDING WITH MY HEAD IN MY HANDS, AND WHILE OUR MEMBERS WERE UN-INSTALLING AND REMOVING THE ITEMS IN OUR BUILDING, I CRIED, AND I ASKED GOD, "SO…WHAT NOW?"

Chapter 6

SO...WHAT NOW?

I THINK GOD WAS WAITING FOR ME TO ASK.

HE WAS BRINGING EVERYTHING I HAD EVER LEARNED ABOUT HIM IN THE 45 YEARS OF WALKING WITH HIM INTO A CLASSROOM CALLED **LIFE'S REVIEW.**

THE REWARD OF REMEMBRANCE...

LET'S SEE WHAT YOU LEARNED ABOUT FAITH. WHAT DO YOU KNOW ABOUT TRUST? WHAT CAN YOU REMEMBER ABOUT HOW I REWARD PERSEVERANCE? WHAT DID DAVID SAY ABOUT NOT BEING FORSAKEN, OR HIS SEED BEGGING FOR BREAD? HEY Y'ALL, I'M NOT TRYING TO SOUND ALL CHURCHY AND STUFF, BUT WHAT WAS INSTILLED AND EMBEDDED IN ME WAS GETTING READY TO COME OUT OF ME. I DISCOVERED A WORD DEEPLY HIDDEN IN MY

HEART THAT GAVE ME A DEGREE OF COMFORT AND EXPECTATION.

BELIEVE IT OR NOT, I WAS GETTING READY TO EXPERIENCE A SIDE OF THE HOLY SPIRIT THAT I DIDN'T HAVE A LOT OF EXPERIENCE WITH ON THIS LEVEL...HE WAS ABOUT TO BRING A WHOLE LOT OF THINGS TO MY REMEMBRANCE... (JOHN 14:26).

WHAT HAVE YOU LEARNED ABOUT MY CHARACTER? WHAT DO YOU KNOW ABOUT ME? I HAVE MANY NAMES, AND ONE OF THEM IS **JEHOVAH - JIREH**; NOT JUST ANOTHER NAME MEANING **PROVIDER**, BUT IT'S THE **PLACE** WHERE GOD IS SEEN OR REVEALED? AND YOU ARE GOING TO SEE ME! DIDN'T I PROCLAIM TO YOU THAT IF I AM FOR YOU, WHO CAN BE AGAINST YOU? **(ROMANS 8:31).** DIDN'T I EXPLAIN TO YOU THAT NO WEAPON FORMED AGAINST YOU WOULD PROSPER

(ISAIAH 54:17), AND THAT EVERY TONGUE THAT RISES UP AGAINST YOU IN JUDGMENT, YOU WILL CONDEMN IT?

OH MY GOD! I WAS FINALLY DISCOVERING HOW TO ALLOW HIM TO RESIDE WITH ME IN THE MIDST OF **MY MEANTIME.**

Chapter 7

PURSUE

HAVE YOU EVER SLIPPED ON ICE AND FELL, AND JUMPED BACK UP QUICKLY TO SAY "I'M OKAY… THAT DIDN'T HURT"; WHEN ALL THE TIME YOU WERE IN SERIOUS PAIN? THEN YOU KNOW WHERE I WAS. UNDER A HUGE MICROSCOPE BEING WATCHED AND STUDIED BY SEEMINGLY EVERYONE.

MY FATHER AND SENIOR PASTOR OF THE HOLY TABERNACLE CHURCH OF GOD IN CHRIST COMFORTED ME WHEN HE OPENED UP THE DOORS OF MY HOME CHURCH, AND WE BEGAN HAVING SERVICES THERE ON SUNDAY AFTERNOONS. MY FATHER, WHO HAS PASTORED THE SAME CHURCH FOR **60 YEARS**, GAVE ME THE KEYS TO THE CHURCH, AND IT WAS LIKE HAVING BEEN ON A LONG VACATION, AND COMING HOME. THIS STORY AND MY LIFE DOESN'T EXIST WITHOUT MY FATHER, PASTOR ROBERT CRISS, AND MY DECEASED MOTHER,

EVANGELIST GEORGIANNA CRISS, UPON WHO'S SHOULDERS I STAND. IT WAS THEIR STERN TEACHING OF UNCOMPROMISING HOLINESS, AND THE TEACHINGS OF RIGHTEOUS LIVING AND FASTING AND PRAYER THAT GOT ME THROUGH. THEY TAUGHT ME HOW TO LAY OUT BEFORE GOD AND SEEK HIS FACE FOR ANSWERS, AND HOW TO HAVE REAL RELATIONSHIP WITH GOD. THEY TAUGHT ME (AND MY 7 SIBLINGS) HOW TO LIVE A COMITTED LIFE UNTO GOD. MY FATHER SHED TEARS IN FRONT OF ME AS HE WOULD SHARE LIFE'S JOYS AND THE WOES OF PASTORAL STRUGGLES WITH ME, AS HE WOULD SAY THINGS LIKE "YOU'LL SEE WHEN YOU BECOME A PASTOR." I'M FOREVER GRATEFUL DAD; THANKS WITH ALL THE LOVE I HAVE IN MY HEART. WITHOUT YOU, THERE'S NO ME; **WHAT LEGENDS...AND MASTERS OF MEANTIMES!**

WE STILL HAD A REMNANT OF CONGREGANTS WHO STAYED, AND HELPED TO KEEP THE CHURCH GOING.WE ALSO HAD PEOPLE WHO

CAME OUT OF BRAZEN CURIOSITY TO SEE IF WE REALLY WERE SURVIVING, AND THAT'S COOL TOO.

THANK GOD, WE WERE NEVER WITHOUT A PLACE TO WORSHIP, AND WE WERE HAVING SOME SERIOUS CHURCH SERVICES WHICH WERE BRINGING US CLOSER TOGETHER.

SOMEHOW, I HAD TO BELIEVE THAT GOD WOULD EXONERATE ME IN HIS OWN TIME, AND NOT LEAVE ME BRANDED AS THE **GAZINGSTOCK OF OUR CITY**.

QUITTING WOULD HAVE BEEN TOO EASY, BUT IT SURE SEEMED LIKE THE BEST RESOLVE. I SAID TO MYSELF, I'M NOT SURE I EVEN WANT TO RECOVER. I WOULD JUST RATHER MOVE ON, WHERE I KNOW NO ONE AND AM KNOWN BY NO ONE. I WAS SURROUNDED BY FRIENDLY FIRE. ONE THING I INTEND TO STRESS AS A PASTOR AND AS A BISHOP IN THE LORD'S CHURCH, IS HOW TO GENUINELY ENCOURAGE FOLKS THAT HAVE REACHED A PLACE IN THEIR JOURNEY WHERE WORDS JUST DON'T WORK. SOMETIMES THE MINISTRY OF PRESENCE IS THE MOST EFFECTIVE THING TO OFFER SOMEONE. IT'S AMAZING TO ME THAT SO MANY HAVE LEARNED THE ART OF DISMANTLING, WHILE FEW HAVE MASTERED THE ART OF REBUILDING; JUST MY OBSERVATION.

SO... I HEADED TO CHICAGO TO SPEND SOME TIME WITH MY BISHOP AND SPIRITUAL FATHER, BISHOP LARRY D. TROTTER, SENIOR PASTOR OF THE SWEET HOLY SPIRIT CHURCH. AS I SAT COMFORTABLY ON THE LIVING ROOM FLOOR, HE SAT IN HIS CHAIR, LISTENING TO ME SPILL EXHAUSTIVELY FOR HOURS. WE HAD PEANUT BUTTER AND SYRUP SANDWICHES WITH

LEMONADE AS WE WENT BACK AND FORTH
WITH ALL OF THE EVENTS WHICH PROMPTED
MY TRAVELS TO SEE HIM. HONESTLY, **I WAS
EMPTY**. I BELIEVED THAT POSSIBLY I HAD
COMPLETED MY ASSIGNMENT IN PEORIA AND
WAS READY TO TAKE MY FAMILY AND HEAD
TO A WARMER CLIMATE, AND, OF COURSE,
FRIENDLIER SURROUNDINGS.

I REMINDED BISHOP TROTTER THAT I HAD
BEEN BLESSED WITH A GOOD EDUCATION AND
A LOT OF VARIED BUSINESS EXPERIENCES THAT
I COULD USE ELSEWHERE (IN THE COUNTRY) IN
MINISTRY, AS I PRESSED HIM FOR HIS WISDOM
AND GUIDANCE. TRUTH IS, I REALLY HAD COME
THERE TO DISCUSS AN EXIT STRATEGY. **I WAS
DONE.**

I THOROUGHLY RESPECTED WHATEVER BISHOP
WOULD SAY, AND EVEN HOPED THAT HE WOULD
CONSIDER RECOMMENDING ME TO ANOTHER
PASTOR OR BISHOP. SINCE MINISTRY IS MY LIFE,
I STILL WANTED THE OPPORTUNITY TO SERVE
GOD'S PEOPLE.

PURSUE

WHAT CAME OUT OF HIS MOUTH WAS A
STARTLING SURPRISE TO ME. I THOUGHT
THAT BISHOP WOULD SIDE WITH ME WITH AN
UNDERSTANDING THAT I HAD TAKEN QUITE
THE BEATING, AND THAT I SHOULD CUT MY

LOSSES, AND MOVE ON. INSTEAD, BISHOP SAID **"I'M SURE YOU COULD SERVE WELL UNDER ANOTHER MINISTRY, AND GOD WOULD PROBABLY ALLOW IT, BUT IT WOULD ONLY BE FOR A SEASON. EVENTUALLY, YOU WILL HAVE TO GET BACK TO THE WILL OF GOD, AND PEORIA IS GOD'S WILL CONCERNING YOU; SO GO BACK TO PEORIA, AND FIGHT TO GET YOUR CHURCH BACK. KEEP THE PEOPLE TOGETHER, AND REBUILD; GOD IS NOT THROUGH WITH YOU, AND YOUR ASSIGNMENT IS NOT COMPLETE!"**

(IT LOOKED TO ME LIKE THIS PLANE WAS GOING TO HAVE TO BE FIXED WHILE IN THE AIR).

NEEDLESS TO SAY, THE DRIVE HOME FROM CHICAGO WAS VERY DIFFICULT. I WAS SO ANGRY WITH BISHOP TROTTER, AND THE LORD, THAT I COULD BARELY CONTAIN MYSELF; I THOUGHT IF ANYBODY WOULD UNDERSTAND ME, BISHOP TROTTER WOULD…HE SHOULD! THE TYPE OF WISDOM THAT BISHOP TROTTER HAS GAINED IS SIMPLY INVALUABLE, AND IT WAS A HUMBLING EXPERIENCE TO BE THE RECIPIENT OF SUCH PERTINENT, INTIMATE INFORMATION FROM A GENERAL IN THE LORD'S CHURCH.

I HAD TO KEEP IN MIND THAT BISHOP WAS THE ONE WHO TOLD ME, AND THE WORLD, **THAT IF WE LOST EVERYTING, BUT STILL HAD JESUS, WE WOULD STILL HAVE ENOUGH TO START OVER AGAIN! I SHOULD HAVE EXPECTED THIS!**

WHAT AN EPIPHANY!...

IT JUST GOT REAL! ALL THIS TIME I'VE BEEN TRYING TO PEN WORDS THAT WOULD GET YOU TO EMPATHIZE WITH ME...TO FEEL ME; WHEN MY SAVIOR WAS TRYING TO GET ME TO FEEL HIM.

I WAS HAVING A REAL JESUS ENCOUNTER, AND DIDN'T RECOGNIZE IT; IT WAS MASKED BY MY SELF-PITY, AND I FELT LIKE I DESERVED TO OWN THAT. I REALLY DID! WHY WAS I BEHAVING LIKE JESUS DIDN'T HAVE A RIGHT TO LET ME EXPERIENCE A **GLIMPSE** OF HOW HE FELT AS HE WAS FACING THE CROSS; AND THAT WAS FOR MY SAKE, FOR MY SALVATION? WHO DID I THINK I WAS TO TRY TO ESCAPE BEING TALKED ABOUT, REJECTED AND SHUNNED, AND MADE TO FEEL UNCOMFORTABLE, UNWANTED, AND UNNECESSARY? THE QUESTION KEPT RESURFACING...WHAT, AND IN WHOM DID I REALLY BELIEVE? THIS AREA OF MY LIFE WAS TRULY BEING TRIED BY FIRE.

SO, THE CLOSER I GOT TO PEORIA, THE MORE RESOLVED I BECAME TO FIGHT FOR WHAT GOD HAD ENTRUSTED TO ME.

WAITING FOR INSTRUCTIONS...

I FIGURED I HAD RECEIVED THE "WHAT?". NOW I DESPERATELY NEEDED THE "HOW?". DURING

THIS SEASON, I WAS SO VERY ATTENTIVE TO THE VOICE OF GOD. I ONLY WANTED TO HEAR INSTRUCTIONS FROM HIM; I ONLY WANTED UNEMOTIONAL CRYSTAL CLEAR DIRECTIONS. AFTER ALL, I WAS IN GOD'S INTENSIVE CARE, AND THIS NEXT MOVE WAS CRUCIAL. EVERY UTTERANCE FROM THE LORD WAS GOING TO BE VITAL, AS MY LIFE, AND THE LIVES OF THOSE ATTACHED TO ME DEPENDED ON IT.

TRYING TO STAY GROUNDED, AND MAKING SOUND DECISIONS WERE ABSOLUTELY ESSENTIAL RIGHT THROUGH HERE.

SO, HE TAUGHT ME AN UNFORGETTABLY, PROFOUND LESSON FROM DAVID'S TESTIMONY IN 1SAMUEL 30.

MY TURNING POINT...

TRIUMPHANTLY, DAVID RETURNED FROM BATTLE TO HIS HOME AT ZIKLAG, ONLY TO FIND THEIR CITY DEMOLISHED BY FIRE, AND THEIR WIVES AND CHILDREN KIDNAPPED BY THEIR ENEMIES; AND THEY'D BEEN MISSING NOW FOR THREE DAYS. AFTER THEY WEPT UNTIL THEIR EYES COULD PRODUCE NO MORE TEARS, THEIR MOURNING TURNED TO ANGER, AND THEY SPOKE OF RETALIATION; NOT AGAINST THEIR ENEMIES, BUT AGAINST DAVID.

IN THE MIDST OF ALL OF THE TURMOIL AND

EMOTIONAL ANGUISH AND CONFUSION, DAVID ENCOURAGED HIMSELF!

DAVID INQUIRED OF GOD, SHOULD WE GO AFTER WHAT BELONGS TO US, AND IF WE DO, WILL WE CATCH UP? GOD REPLIED, **"PURSUE"** AND YOU WILL NOT ONLY OVERTAKE THEM, **BUT WITHOUT FAIL, RECOVER ALL.**

EVEN WHEN HIS COMRADES GREW TOO WEAK TO CONTINUE THE JOURNEY, AND COULDN'T GO ANY FURTHER THAN THE BROOK (OF BESOR), DAVID TOOK STRENGTH, PUSHED FORWARD, AND **PURSUED.**

I UNDERSTAND NOW THAT SYMBOLICALLY, THE BROOK WAS AS FAR AS SOME HAD THE CAPACITY TO GO; SO I COULD NOT HARBOR ANGER FOR THOSE WHO COULDN'T CONTINUE. THANK GOD FOR ALL WHO DARED TO SOJOURN.

WITH UNWAVERING CONFIDENCE, DAVID CONSOLED HIMSELF THAT GOD WOULD BRING **COMPLETE** VICTORY AND RECOVERY.

IN HIS OMNISCIENCE, GOD LEVELED THE PLAYING FIELD WHEN HE ARRESTED AN EXHAUSTED, HUNGRY SERVANT WHO KNEW THE WHEREABOUTS OF DAVID'S ENEMIES AND HIS BELONGINGS; AND DAVID HAD SOMETHING THAT THE SERVANT DESPERATELY NEEDED; FOOD AND REFRESHMENTS. AND THUS, **THE GREAT**

EXCHANGE TOOK PLACE. THIS EXCHANGE ONLY HAPPENED BECAUSE DAVID DARED TO PURSUE.

BASED ON THE INTELLIGENCE RECEIVED, DAVID WAS ABLE TO FINE TUNE HIS DIRECTIONS, REDEEM THE THREE DAY HEADSTART HIS ENEMIES HAD ENJOYED, CATCH AND DESTROY HIS ENEMY, AND RECUPERATE HIS LOSSES.

IN FACT, WHAT HE BROUGHT HOME WAS NOT ONLY WHAT HAD BEEN TAKEN FROM HIM, BUT TREASURES THAT HAD BEEN STOLEN FROM OTHERS.NOT ONLY DID HE COME HOME RESTORED, HE WAS EQUIPPED TO RESTORE OTHERS!

MEANTIMES HAVE **PURPOSE.**OFTEN THEY ARE DISGUISED AS UNPRODUCTIVE TIMES; BUT WHEN GOD IS DONE, AND THE REVELATION IS CLEAR, YOU REALIZE IT WAS GAIN TIME. YOU MADE REMARKABLE ADVANCES DURING THIS TIME. YOU GREW AND PROSPERED BECAUSE YOU ENDURED WHAT YOU COULD HAVE VERY EASILY WALKED AWAY FROM.

I'M CONVINCED WE OFTEN FORFEIT OPPORTUNITIES TO WORSHIP HIM, BECAUSE WE ARE UNAWARE OF THE VALUE OF WHAT GOD IS PERFORMING FOR US BEHIND THE SCENES. JUST TAKE A MOMENT TO THANK HIM FOR WHAT HE HAS HELPED YOU TO ENDURE; AFTER ALL, YOU LIVED **THROUGH** WHAT SOME

FOLKS DIED **IN.** THANK HIM FOR PEOPLE THAT CONTRIBUTED TO YOUR JOURNEY, WHETHER GOOD OR BAD. THANK HIM FOR THAT WHICH YOUR ENEMY CAREFULLY ORCHESTRATED FOR YOUR DEMISE; BUT IT FAILED MISERABLY, AND WAS TURNED AROUND TO WORK FOR YOUR GOOD.

TAKE A MOMENT TO LISTEN TO THE SONG THAT GOD GAVE ME WHICH ACCOMPANIES THIS BOOK CALLED "STILL STANDING". LET IT BLESS YOU NOW!

"FOR **OUR LIGHT AFFLICTION, WHICH IS BUT FOR A MOMENT, WORKS FOR US A FAR MORE EXCEEDING AND ETERNAL WEIGHT OF GLORY"** (II COR 4:17).

LIKE DAVID, I WAS INSPIRED TO PURSUE!

Chapter 8

RE-POSSESS THE LAND

I HOPE YOU HAD A CHANCE TO LISTEN TO AND BE BLESSED BY THE LYRICS OF THE SONG "STILL STANDING." I ALSO PRAY IT WILL CONTINUALLY BLESS YOU AS YOU SHARE IT WITH OTHERS.

IT WAS NOW TIME TO ROLL UP OUR SLEEVES, GO TO WORK, AND BE ABOUT THE BUSINESS OF RECLAIMING WHAT WAS OURS.

OUR FACILITY WAS NOW LISTED BY RE-MAX, AND WE HAD BEEN TOLD THAT SEVERAL ENTITIES HAD EXPRESSED INTEREST IN PURCHASING THE BUILDING. ONE BIBLE STUDY NIGHT, ONE OF OUR DEACONS TOLD ME HE PASSED BY AND NOTICED AN **AUCTION** SIGN ON THE BUILDING ALONGSIDE THE **FOR SALE** SIGN. THESE PUBLIC DISPLAYS WERE DAUNTING TO OUR PEOPLE, AS HOPES OF RECLAIMING OUR BUILDING SEEMED TO FADE. HOWEVER, **WE CONTINUED TO PURSUE. OUR PEOPLE CAME TOGETHER IN AN**

UNPRECEDENTED MANNER TO RAISE FUNDS, ANTICIPATING THAT WE MAY HAVE A CHANCE AT THE AUCTION.

AFTER A PERIOD OF TIME, WE CALLED THE AUCTION HOUSE AND REQUESTED A VISIT TO SEE THE CHURCH PRIOR TO THE AUCTION.

WITHOUT TELLING THEM WHO WE WERE, WE WALKED THROUGH ALL THE FAMILIAR AREAS OF THE BUILDING WITH TEARS IN OUR EYES WHILE REMINISCING. A WATER PIPE HAD BURST, AND CAUSED SERIOUS WATER DAMAGE ON THE MAIN FLOOR, AND THE LOWER LEVEL. WE DIDN'T CARE; WE JUST WANTED TO BE HOME. OUR BUILDING WAS BROKEN AND DISMANTLED. IT WAS COLD, SMELLY, AND DIRTY; KIND OF LIKE IT WAS WHEN WE FIRST PURCHASED IT.

WE HAD ALSO ENTERED INTO DISCUSSIONS WITH A DEAR FRIEND OF OUR MINISTRY WHO AGREED TO ASSIST US IN RE-POSSESSING OUR BUILDING.

THE EVENING BEFORE...

IT HAD BEEN THE SWIRL OF THE CITY THAT OUR BUILDING WAS UP FOR AUCTION SCHEDULED FOR THE NEXT DAY. I RECEIVED A CALL FROM A REPORTER ASKING IF WE WERE GOING TO ATTEND. OF COURSE, I REPLIED THAT WE WOULD BE IN ATTENDANCE. I SAID

TO HIM THAT HE REALLY SHOULD WAIT UNTIL THE DAY AFTER THE AUCTION TO REPORT HIS STORY. I THOUGHT THAT WOULD MAKE MORE SENSE. HE ANSWERED, YOU LOST EVERYTHING YOU HAD INCLUDING YOUR BUSINESSES, YOUR HOUSE, YOUR CARS, AND NOW THE CHURCH; **AND THAT'S NEWS!**

THE MORNING OF...

I WAS AWAKENED ABOUT 6A.M. I HEARD THE VOICE OF THE LORD SAY "TODAY, I'M GOING TO SHOW YOU THAT I'M WITH YOU!"

YOU SHOULD HAVE HEARD ME PRAISING GOD FOR HIS COMMUNICATION WITH ME. I KNEW I HAD HEARD FROM GOD. THIS IS WHAT I'D BEEN WAITING FOR. OUR PURSUIT WAS NOT IN VAIN. I DIDN'T KNOW HOW THIS WOULD MANIFEST; I JUST MOVED WITH CONFIDENCE. I WAS SO LOUD, I THINK I AWAKENED EVERYBODY IN THE HOUSE. I WENT TO BURLINGTON COAT FACTORY AND BOUGHT A NEW SHIRT, AND IRONED MY JEANS LIKE I WAS IN THE MARINES, AND GOT READY FOR THE AUCTION. ON THE WAY I PICKED UP A NEWSPAPER, AND FOUND OUR STORY WAS THE FIRST STORY ON THE **FRONT PAGE.** I COULDN'T BUY THAT MANY PAPERS! COME ON Y'ALL...**THE FRONT PAGE?!** I COULD SAY MORE, BUT IT'S NOT MORE SENSATIONAL THAN WHAT I'M ABOUT TO TELL YOU. FASTEN UP, GET READY; IT'S GOING TO BLESS YOU.

I MOVED WITH HASTE, AS THE HOUR WAS QUICKLY APPROACHING FOR THE AUCTION. A MIRACLE WAS ABOUT TO HAPPEN! I COULD FEEL IT IN THE MAKING. AS SOON AS I AND SEVERAL OF OUR PEOPLE GOT THERE, WE NOTICED NEWS TRUCKS, REPORTERS, AND CAMERAS. WHY? **AT AN AUCTION!?** EITHER THE DEVIL WAS GOING TO TRY TO ADD MORE INSULT TO INJURY, OR GOD WAS GETTING READY TO BROADCAST HOW POWERFUL HE WAS AND DEMONSTRATE HIS FAVOR, IN LIVING COLOR, AND I WAS GOING TO BE ONE OF THE WITNESSES IN THE NEWS STORY. EITHER WAY, I HAD A FRONT ROW SEAT!

I'VE BEEN TO AUCTIONS BEFORE...THERE WERE NO CAMERAS, NO REPORTERS, ETC. WELL, IF NOTHING ELSE, I LOOKED INTERVIEW- READY!

OUR FACILITY WAS FIRST ON THE LIST TO BE AUCTIONED. AND THERE SHE WAS IN ALL OF HER SPLENDOR, AND DISREPAIR. AS THE AUCTIONEER DESCRIBED OUR BUILDING, AND ALL OF THE RENOVATIONS WITH FRENCH DOORS AND NEW LIGHTING, MODERN HEATING AND AIR CONDITIONING, CARPETED FLOORS AND ETC., MY HEART SWELLED WITH THE THOUGHT OF GOING HOME AS THE RE-POSSESSORS OF OUR PROPERTY.

I, AND OUR FRIEND, GAVE THE OPENING BID. THEN SOMEONE COUNTERED. I WAS TOO INTENSE TO LOOK BEHIND ME TO SEE WHO

IT WAS. SO THEN, I COUNTERED BACK, ONLY TO HEAR ANOTHER OFFER BEHIND ME. I COUNTERED AGAIN, AND THERE WAS NO RESPONSE; EXCEPT FOR THE AUCTIONEER YELLING **"SOLD TO THE GENTLEMAN UP FRONT."**

I WAS TRYING TO BEHAVE AS IF I WASN'T SURPRISED, LIKE I HAD DONE THIS BEFORE; BUT WHEN I HEARD OUR PEOPLE IN THE REAR OF THE ROOM CELEBRATING, I HAD TO JOIN THEM IN PRAISE. MY FRIEND AND I HAD TO GO AND TAKE CARE OF THE BUSINESS AT HAND TO WRAP THINGS UP, BUT WHEN WE FINISHED, WE HAD

AGREED WITH THE BANK AS TO WHEN WE COULD TAKE **RE-POSSESSION** OF OUR FACILITY.

OUR MEMBERS MET ME ON THE SIDEWALK OF OUR CHURCH FACILITY THAT EVENING AND WE SANG, SHOUTED, PRAISED AND WORSHIPPED UNTIL WE GOT TIRED. THE BANK REPORTED THAT WE HAD OWED OVER $1,000.000.00. WE RE-PURCHASED OUR FACILITY FOR APPROXIMATELY A TITHE (I WILL LET YOU TITHERS FIGURE THAT ONE OUT.) TO EVERYONE READING THIS THAT DOESN'T FEEL THE NECESSITY TO TITHE, LET THIS BE YOUR TIME OF REPENTANCE, AND YOUR NEW FOUND COMITTMENT FROM THIS DAY FORWARD; **EFFECTIVE IMMEDIATELY!**

GOD HAD DONE WHAT HE ALWAYS DOES…HE RAISED OUR BOWED HEADS; HE REWARDED OUR FAITH; HE LIFTED OUR SPIRITS; HE RESTORED OUR PUBLIC RESPECT; HE HONORED OUR PRAYERS; HE KEPT HIS PROMISE! GOD HAD PLACED US ON THE ROAD TO RECOVERY; AND I KEPT MINE: I DANCED BEFORE THE LORD IN THE MIDDLE OF ADAMS STREET, ONLY STOPPING WHEN TRAFFIC WAS PRESENT.

I WALKED OUT OF THE ROOM TO A NUMBER OF CAMERAS AND REPORTERS. I DON'T REALLY REMEMBER THEIR QUESTIONS. I JUST REMEMBER MY RESPONSE; **BUT GOD!**

THE MORNING AFTER…

THE TELEVISION NEWS ANCHOR STARTED HIS TELECAST WITH "CITY OF REFUGE WAS SOLD AT AUCTION YESTERDAY…TO CITY OF REFUGE."

AS A SIDE NOTE, WE MADE THE FRONT PAGE AGAIN, BUT THE LETTERS WEREN'T AS BIG; AND WE WEREN'T THE FIRST STORY EITHER. WHO CARES… **BUT GOD!**

Chapter 9

TIME TO REBUILD...

SO, THE NEXT DAY, MY PERSONAL ASSIGMENT WAS TO CLIMB A LADDER, AND TAKE DOWN THE **AUCTION** SIGN, AND DISMANTLE THE **REMAX FOR SALE SIGN**, AND LEFT THEM FOR PICK-UP.

MY SENIOR DEACON, GOD REST HIS SOUL, DEACON JOE DIXON SAID LET'S CLEAN THE PLACE UP AND HAVE CHURCH; WORDS TO LIVE BY. THESE WERE ALSO THE WORDS THAT FRAMED OUR NEXT ACTIONS. SO MUCH HAD TO BE DONE TO REPAIR THE WATER DAMAGE AND OTHER THINGS THAT, IT BROUGHT OUR PEOPLE TOGETHER LIKE CRAZY. OUR PEOPLE HAD A NEW ENERGY, AND NEW PEP IN THEIR SPIRITS. LIKE BEFORE, THE SAW DUST BEGAN TO FLY, HAMMERS BEGAN TO POUND, AND THE SMELL OF DRYWALL COMPOUND AND FRESH PAINT FILLED THE AIR. IT WAS STARTING TO

LOOK LIKE OUR OLD CHURCH AGAIN, WITH SOMETHING EXTRA.

MY DETERMINATION AS A PASTOR WAS THAT OUR PEOPLE BE REBUILT, JUST AS OUR BUILDING WAS. WE WERE HOME, AND WE WERE STILL A FLOURISHING, GROWING FAMILY.

WE'RE GROWING AND WE'RE GROWING...

WHAT FOLLOWS IS TO GIVE GOD GLORY; NOT FOR BOASTING OF OURSELVES, OR WHAT WE MAY HAVE ACCOMPLISHED BY OUR OWN HANDS. IT'S THE LORD'S DOING, AND IT IS MARVELOUS IN OUR EYES. HE HAS BLESSED US WITH SEVERAL NEW PERSONAL AND COMMUNITY PROJECTS TO PURSUE:

THE CHURCH IS GROWING NUMERICALLY...

SHERRY AND I HAVE PURCHASED A HOME EVEN MORE

BEAUTIFUL THAN THE ONE WE LOST...

WE ARE PURCHASING VACANT PROPERTY IMMEDIATELY ACROSS THE STREET FROM THE CHURCH FOR FUTURE EXPANSION...

WE ALSO HAVE OTHER PROPERTY A BLOCK AWAY FROM THE CHURCH WHICH WAS WILLED TO US...

WE ACQUIRED TWO ADDITIONAL BUILDINGS A BLOCK FROM THE CHURCH...ONE WE SOLD, AND THE OTHER WE TRADED...

THE TRADE WAS FOR THE PURCHASE OF OUR 66,000 SQUARE FOOT SCHOOL BUILDING THAT SITS ON 3.5 ACRES, AND HOUSES TWO GYMNASIUMS AND A SCIENCE LAB. WE CALL IT P**ROMISE ACADEMY**, AND OUR GOAL IS TO BE OPEN BY THE FALL OF 2017. OUR SCHOOL IS LOCATED SIX BLOCKS FROM THE CHURCH, AND IS IN THE HEART OF OUR RESIDENTIAL AND BUSINESS COMMUNITY.

WE'RE ALSO WORKING WITH THE LARGEST HOSPITAL IN OUR CITY TO BRING A FAMILY HEALTH CLINIC TO OUR SCHOOL BUILDING (2017).

(THERE ARE SEVERAL OTHER PROJECTS THAT I'M NOT PREPARED TO UNCOVER AT THE TIME OF THIS NARRATIVE).

I'M SO GLAD WE CHOSE TO PURSUE!

Chapter 10

SO...WHAT DID I LEARN ABOUT MEANTIMES...

SOMETIMES GOD SAYS "AGAIN"...

IN MY YOUNGER YEARS, I PLAYED THE SAXAPHONE AND DRUMS IN MY HIGH SCHOOL BAND. AFTER HOURS AND HOURS OF PRACTICE YOU COULD HEAR THE PARTS COMING TOGETHER, WHICH MADE THE DIRECTOR PROUD. OFTEN, JUST AS WE PLAYED A PIECE THAT SOUNDED GREAT TO US, HE WOULD STOP US AND SAY "AGAIN." I WOULD ASK MYSELF, WHAT WAS WRONG WITH THAT? THEN IN HUMBLE DEFIANCE, LIFT MY INSTRUMENT IN PREPARATION TO PLAY IT AGAIN. MOST TIMES, I WAS ONLY CONCERNED ABOUT OUR SECTION'S PARTS, WHILE THE DIRECTOR'S EAR WAS TRAINED TO HEAR THE ENTIRE SCORE. OF COURSE, HE ALSO YELLED "AGAIN" WHEN IT WAS CORRECT, AND HE WAS INVITING US TO

HEAR WHAT PERFECTION SOUNDED LIKE, SO WE WOULDN'T FORGET IT, SINCE IT CAME AS A REWARD OF OUR PERSISTENCE, AND LABOR.

IN JEREMIAH CHAPTER 18, THE POTTER MADE THE VESSEL AGAIN WHEN IT WAS DISCOVERED THAT THERE WAS A FLAW IN IT. HE RE-MADE IT UNTIL HE WAS PLEASED WITH WHAT HE HAD MADE, EVEN IF IT WAS ANOTHER VESSEL ALL TOGETHER.GOD RESERVES THE RIGHT AS THE POTTER TO ADJUST US, SHAPE US, AND PUT HIS FINGER PRINTS ON US ACCORDING TO HIS PURPOSE. IT'S OK IF HE SHOULD ELECT TO CRUSH US, AND MAKE US AGAIN. AFTER ALL, WE BELONG TO HIM. MAYBE YOUR VESSEL WAS BROKEN FOR **INCREASE.**

DON'T DIE WHILE YOU'RE WAITING…

MEANTIMES TRY EVERYTHING YOU'RE MADE OF. YOUR ABILITY TO WAIT ON THE LORD WITH PATIENCE IS ESSENTIAL. GOD IS THE MASTER OF TIME, AND HE IS NOT RUSHED BY OUR IMPATIENCE, NOR INTIMIDATED BY OUR ATTEMPTS TO PURSUADE HIM TO MOVE BEFORE HIS SET TIME. SCRIPTURE PROVES THAT GOD UTILIZES SEASONS (ECCLESIASTES 3), AND WE MUST LEARN NOT TO BECOME WEARY IN WELL DOING, FOR IN DUE SEASON, WE'LL REAP A BOUNTIFUL HARVEST…JUST DON'T FAINT.

DON'T LET WHERE YOU ARE MAKE YOU

ANXIOUS ABOUT WHERE YOU'RE GOING. RESIST BECOMING BITTER BY KEEPING YOUR WORSHIP LIFE IN TACT. REMEMBER, REAL WORSHIP IS EXTRAVAGANT LOVE, MINGLED WITH EXTREME SURRENDER. KNOW THAT YOUR STEPS ARE ORDERED BY HIM; AND IF YOUR STEPS ARE ORDERED, THEN SO ARE YOUR TEST, TRIAL, AND TRIUMPHS.

ISAIAH 40:31 RECORDS "THEY THAT WAIT UPON THE LORD SHALL RENEW YOUR STRENGTH… YOU READ IT…IT'S THERE FOR YOU.

TROUBLES DON'T LAST ALWAYS…

SO OUT-LAST YOUR TROUBLES. REMEMBER, AND TRUST THAT SCRIPTURE DECLARES II CORINTHIANS 4:18…WHAT CAN BE SEEN IS TEMPORARY, AND WHAT IS NOT SEEN IS ETERNAL. FOCUS ON THE ETERNAL BENEFITS THAT SHALL BE REVEALED IN YOUR LIFE. IT'S WORKING FOR YOU, AND IT'S WORKING FOR YOUR GOOD (ROMANS 8:28).

WELCOME YOUR TEARS. RELEASE THAT PRESSURE, AND LET IT OUT. YOU'RE BEING CLEANSED AND REFRESHED. JUST KNOW THAT SOON, THOSE TEARS WILL BECOME TEARS OF JOY. SOON, YOU'LL BE TRADING YOUR ASHES FOR BEAUTY. ALWAYS REMEMBER, WEEPING MAY ENDURE FOR A NIGHT, BUT JOY IS ON THE

HORIZON OF YOUR MORNING. JUST ENDURE THE NIGHT!

THE GRACE TO RECOVER...THE POWER TO BOUNCE BACK

THE SILVER LINING THAT COMES WITH EVERY STORM OF ADVERSITY IS THE ABILITY TO RECOVER. MANY ARE THE AFFLICTIONS OF THE RIGHTEOUS, BUT THE LORD DELIVERS HIM OUT OF THEM **ALL.** TAKE COURAGE THAT YOU'RE NOT STRANDED, BUT YOU'RE GAINING MOMENTUM AS YOU KEEP MOVING.

YOU'RE GOING TO MAKE MISTAKES, BUT MISTAKES HAPPEN BECAUSE YOU'RE DOING SOMETHING. YOU HAVE BEEN GIVEN THAT GRACE TO TURN AROUND, AND MAKE IT RIGHT. DON'T SPEND ALL YOUR TIME ADDING UP YOUR ERRORS. START PLANNING YOUR RISE WHEN YOU FALL. SAY TO YOURSELF, THIS WILL NOT BE THE FINAL CHAPTER IN MY BOOK. YOU'RE TOO CLOSE TO YOUR BOUNCEBACK; TOO CLOSE TO YOUR REVELATION; TOO CLOSE TO OVERCOMING THIS TEMPORARY SETBACK. SO GET UP AND SAY "I SHALL NOT DIE, BUT LIVE, AND DECLARE THE WORKS OF THE LORD (PSALMS 118:17).

PLEASE CONSIDER THIS: ACCORDING TO PSALMS 4:1, DAVID DECLARED THAT GOD **ENLARGED** HIM IN DISTRESS...LET GOD DO THE SAME FOR

YOU IN YOUR MEANTIME. YOU CAN'T LOSE MORE THAN WHAT GOD CAN RESTORE.

ALSO, DON'T BE OVERWHELMED BY THE FOLKS WHO CATCH A DANGEROUSLY CONTAGIOUS DISEASE CALLED "ITDONTMATTERWHATYOU-SAYYOUMUSTHAVEDONESOMETHINGWRONGI-TIS"; JOB FRIEND SYNDROME FOR SHORT.

THIS EPIDEMIC CAUSES SELECTIVE VISION THAT ONLY GOES AWAY WHEN THE CONTRACTEE HAS SOMETHING GO AWRY IN THEIR PERSONAL LIVES. THE SIDE EFFECT PROFILE IS QUITE BROAD, BUT IS NOT LIMITED TO HARDENING OF THE HEART, INSENSITIVITY, NARROW MINDEDNESS, INTENSE TONGUE WAGGING, AND SEVERE UNCONTROLLED BLURTS OF CRITICISM. COMPASSION DISAPPEARS. THIS DISEASE MURDERS THE SPIRIT OF HOPE, AND DWARFS GROWTH. IT RUINS MORALE AND TARNISHES REPUTATIONS. IT ALSO FOSTERS DISTRUST, AND CAUSES SEVERE EMOTIONAL WOUNDS.

DO YOU KNOW ANYONE WITH THIS DISORDER? YOU WOULDN'T HAVE IT, WOULD YOU? PLEASE AVOID THIS AT ALL COST. WARNING...IT IS CONTAGIOUS!

THE GOOD NEWS IS YOU CAN BE HEALED BY THE POWER OF GOD; JUST ASK HIM.

IT IS NOT THE WILL OF GOD THAT WE AS BELIEVERS TAKE PART IN TERRORISTIC ACTS, LIKE KILLING OUR WOUNDED. LET'S LEARN TO BE AGENTS OF REBUILDING, RESTORING, ENCOURAGING, AND RECONCILING. THIS WOULD CERTAINLY PLEASE THE LORD. THIS SHOULD BE THE FOCUS OF EVERY MINISTRY.

DURING YOUR MEANTIME, DON'T TRY TO PROVE WHO YOU ARE TO ANYONE, OR MAKE ANYONE CHANGE THEIR MIND ABOUT YOU. IT'S HARD TO THINK BIG WHEN LITTLE HAS YOU! SOMETIMES PEOPLE CAN ONLY PERCEIVE YOU BASED ON WHAT THEY'VE SEEN; AND SOMETIMES THAT'S NOT MUCH.

IT'S AN UNUSUAL PLACE TO BE (FOR YOU AND THEM), WHEN YOUR CIRCUMSTANCES HAVE FORCED YOUR DESIRES AND PERSPECTIVES TO CHANGE. YOUR APETITE CHANGES TOO. SO DON'T BE SHOCKED WHEN SOME OF YOUR FRIENDSHIPS SUFFER AND BECOME STRAINED WHEN THEY CAN'T WALK WHERE GOD HAS YOU WALKING. I'M NOT BEING ELEVATED OR CONDESCENDING; JUST KNOW THAT THIS IS REALLY A CHALLENGE AND A CALL FOR YOU TO WALK MORE CLOSELY TO HIM.

FINALLY, DON'T TRY TO FIX YOUR PAST...IT'S TOO COSTLY, AND IT WASTES TOO MUCH VALUABLE TIME. YOU NEED TO FOCUS ON WHAT LIES AHEAD. DON'T CONTINUE TO

MAKE PEOPLE A PRIORITY WHO MAKE YOU AN OPTION. PLEASE HEAR ME WHEN I TELL YOU, **KEEP MOVING!**

THANK YOU SO MUCH FOR ALLOWING ME THE HONOR OF SHARING THIS PART OF MY LIFE WITH YOU. I SINCERELY PRAY THAT THIS DISCOURSE WILL ASSIST YOU IN WALKING BOLDLY AND VICTORIOUSLY THE NEXT TIME YOU EXPERIENCE ADVERSITY. WHEN OUR PATHS CROSS, I CERTAINLY HOPE THAT YOUR TESTIMONY WILL BE THAT YOU ARE "STILL STANDING" IN THE MIDST OF YOUR MEANTIME.

MY PRAYER FOR YOU IS THAT GOD'S BOUNTIFUL BLESSINGS OVERTAKE YOU, AND HIS LOVE COMFORT YOU, AND GIVE YOU PEACE…AND IT IS SO…

AMEN

BISHOP TIMOTHY E. CRISS

SENIOR PASTOR, GREATER CITY OF REFUGE

PEORIA, ILLINOIS

Printed in the United States
By Bookmasters